T0132367

Dedicated to the memories of Maya Miller, Peg Wheat, Eric McClary, and Wuzzie George.

With many thanks for help and suggestions to Daniel Dixon, Matt Friday, Virginia Fry, Elizabeth Partridge, Greg Raven, Sharkey Roberts, Taelen Thomas, and Linda Yamane. Extra special thanks to amazing storyteller Carol Collin. Grateful appreciation to Andrea Rossman and friends at the Churchill County Museum in Fallon, Nevada, for their help and encouragement.

Our mission is to efficiently provide the world's finest, most comprehensive book publishing
service, enabling every author to experience success. To find out how to publish your book,
your way, and have it available worldwide, visit us online at www.trafford.com

Trafford rev. 07/20/2018

 www.trafford.com
North America & international
toll-free: 1 888 232 4444 (USA & Canada)
fax: 812 355 4082

Foreword

Two remarkable women and a small boy were, in different ways, the inspiration for this book. It is the story of Wuzzie George, an old Paiute Indian woman, who for many years showed children at a summer camp how her people lived and survived in the Northwest region of Nevada.

The other woman was Peg Wheat, a geologist in Nevada's Great Basin area, who discovered that very little had been recorded of the Native Americans living in Western Nevada. With cameras and a recorder, she began spending hours with the Paiutes who inhabited the desert near her home in Fallon, Nevada. They were called the Cattail Eaters. These new Indian friends patiently told and retold stories for her about their daily lives in the inhospitable desert.

By the time the Washoe Pines Summer Camp began in 1962 near Carson City, Peg and Wuzzie were good friends. Peg could speak the Paiute language and she was studying to become an anthropologist.

Peg hired on as the cook for the new summer camp and thought the campers might enjoy meeting Wuzzie. They did. And Wuzzie must have enjoyed meeting the children because she came to the camp each year for many years to show them Paiute ways.

Wuzzie spoke little English so Peg served as her interpreter, but she seemed to understand more English than she claimed because she giggled when someone said something funny.

The discovery of a short journal written many years ago by one of the campers, then nine-year-old Eric McClary, inspired me to write and illustrate this book so other children could enjoy and learn from Wuzzie's story.

I had been a counselor for years at Washoe Pines Camp and knew how much children enjoyed Wuzzie showing them the Paiute Indians' way of living in the desert. Reading Eric's journal made me realize what an unusual and valuable experience it had been to be taught by an Indian who actually lived the stories she told.

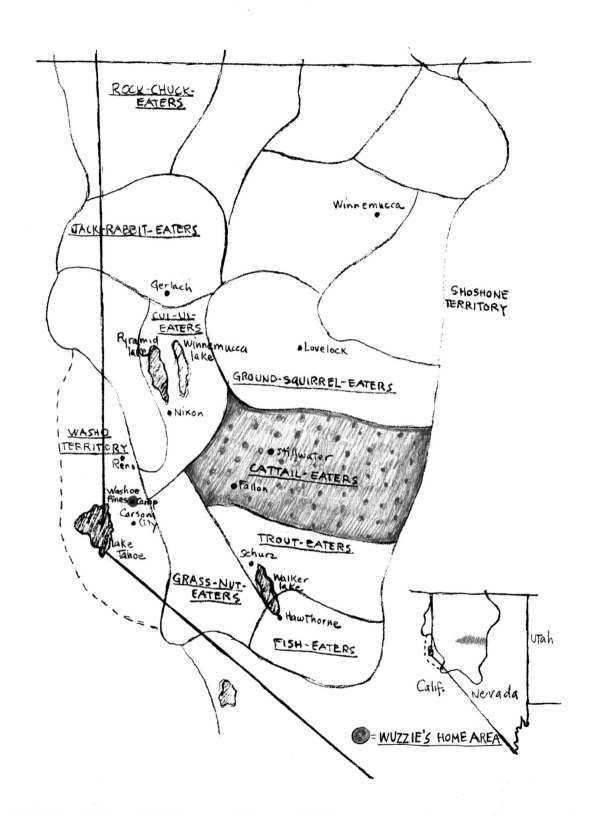

Wuzzie Comes
to Camp

Written and illustrated by Nancy Raven

Washoe Pines Camp

The best part of my summer comes when I go to a camp called Washoe Pines, in the high desert of western Nevada. We sleep in teepees, which are tall cone-shaped tents made out of canvas. They are decorated with petroglyph designs, showing the animals that people hunted long ago. When the sun hits the teepees, the dusty smell reminds me of my Grandma's attic in the summer.

Around the teepees, our feet crunch over pine needles and crisp, dry twigs. The sky is a deep blue, and peeks through the branches of enormous Jeffrey pines which stand like silent, tall giants sheltering the camp. The pungent trees smell sharp and sweet at the same time. I press my nose against the bark, inhaling a smell that's just like vanilla ice cream.

Wuzzie and Peg

Every summer Wuzzie George, a Paiute (PIE-yoot) Indian woman from Stillwater, Nevada, comes to our camp near Carson City. She is about 75 years old and isn't a camper like we are. She comes to show us how her people lived. This story is about some of the ways they got food. Our friend Peg Wheat and Wuzzie have known each other for a long time and Wuzzie has shown Peg many things about how the Paiutes lived.

Peg and Wuzzie arrive early one morning in Peg's old VW camper. We have been watching since breakfast for the cloud of dust that will tell us they are here. We all rush outside and sure enough, Peg's camper is piled high with tules (TOO-lees) and cattails. Peg had driven to Stillwater to pick up Wuzzie and when they turn into the camp's long dirt driveway you can see Wuzzie riding shotgun in her bright red dress.

Wuzzie stays at camp for two days with Peg. They bring lots of neat stuff to share with us. The camper is full of desert plants, seeds, and pine nuts. Cattails and tules are tied on top. Peg's big gray wolf-dog, Silver, sits squashed between all the supplies they have brought. We pile all over the camper to help unload. Peg tells us, "Tules in one pile, cattails in another ... baskets over here, plants and grasses there." Finally everything is unloaded near the fire ring. Silver stretches her legs and investigates the camp.

Peg is older than my Grandma. She's short and squat with white wavy hair. Her skin is weathered and brown, like old leather. Her bright blue eyes are the color of the desert sky, and crinkle in smiles even when her mouth is serious.

Wuzzie's long black hair shines like a raven's wing. It's pulled back and tied with a soft purple scarf. Wuzzie loves bright colors, and always wears dresses. This time she is wearing a deep red dress with purple designs. Her round brown face has twinkling eyes and quizzical little eyebrows. She finds a picnic table and sits down while one of the counselors helps some of us build a small fire so Wuzzie can cook. As soon as the sweet smell of the wood smoke drifts through camp, everyone settles around the fire. I wonder what she will do first. Peg tell us that Wuzzie will start by making rice grass and buckwheat mush.

Rice Grass and Buckwheat Mush

I watch the old woman more carefully than I did in other years. I'm older now and interested in every detail of what she shows us.

Wuzzie begins to work with the dried plants. She rubs rice grass plants between her hands. The seeds and leaves drop into a winnowing basket. It is fan-shaped and very light. Now she is ready to winnow. To winnow, Wuzzie stands up to see where the wind is coming from by turning her face one way and then the other. When she finds the wind, she turns her back to it and tosses the seeds gently into the air. The breeze makes the leaves and twigs fall away from the basket. The seeds are heavier and fall back into the basket. Wuzzie picks out the remaining twigs by hand. She places a handful of the rice grass seeds on a metate (muh-TAH-tay), which is a big, heavy, flat rock. She grinds them gently with another rock she hold in her hands, called a mano (MAH-no). It looks like a baking potato, worn smooth from years of use. Peg explains that rice grass seeds have a sharp husk, or covering, which must be removed before the seed can be used.

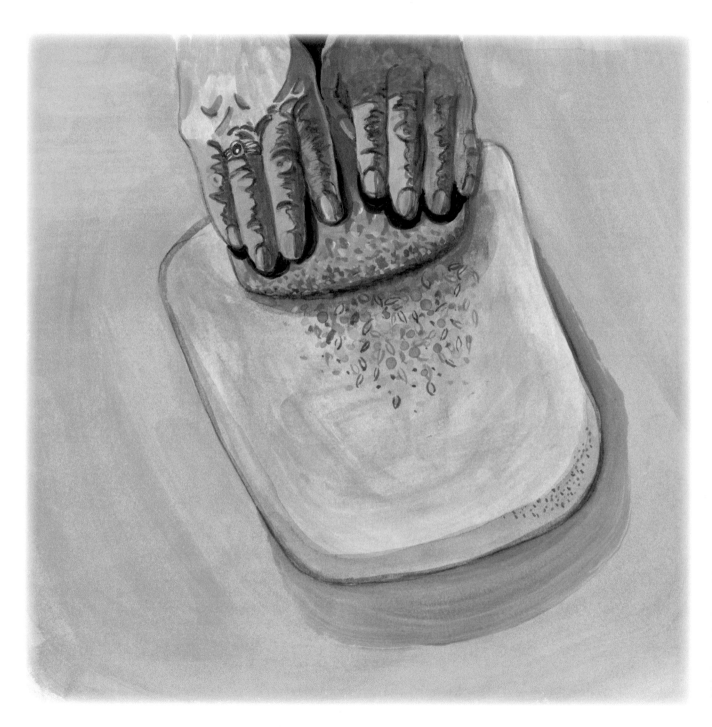

This gentle grinding cracks the sharp husk. After grinding, she is ready to winnow the seeds to get rid of the husks. We all scramble to our feet and follow her to an opening in the trees. Wuzzie checks the wind again, and tosses the seeds gently into the air. Her back is straight and strong, and her movements are slow and graceful. She shakes the seeds in the basket up and down and sideways. The breeze carries away the husks while the heavier seeds remain in the basket. Wuzzie shows us the cleaned seeds which are no bigger than the head of a pin, and I wonder how the Paiutes discovered that this was food.

Wuzzie sets the rice grass seeds aside in a small basket, and does the same thing with some of the buckwheat seeds. They are soft and fuzzy, and very different from the rice grass seeds. This time when she winnows, she is getting rid of tiny twigs and leaves. Finally they are all cleaned, and she puts them together on the metate, and grinds the seeds into a fine brown flour. Now she carefully scrapes the flour into a bowl-basket and adds some cold water. She stirs it with a stick into a mush that the Paiutes eat a lot. Wuzzie smiles in amusement as we stick our fingers into the mush to taste it. It's good, but it has a plain, bland taste, and I look forward to the taste of the pine nut soup she makes. I hope she does that next. But then the lunch bell rings, and Peg says we will do the pine nuts later. She takes Wuzzie back to her camper where they eat lunch together and rest. We head to the kitchen hall for peanut butter sandwiches and fruit, and I wonder what interesting things Peg and Wuzzie are having for lunch.

Pine Nut Soup

After rest time, the air is warmer, and we crowd around the fire pit, sitting on the dusty ground. Wuzzie is stirring up the coals from the morning fire which are still hot and glowing. Next to Wuzzie is a basketful of pine nuts. Pine nut soup is next!!

Peg and Wuzzie have brought these pine nuts from last fall's harvest. Harvesting pine nuts is hard work. Peg tells us that the Paiutes use a long pole to knock the cones off the piñon (PIN-yon) pine trees. After the cones are gathered off the ground they are put in a hot fire pit to make them open. It is hard work removing the nuts from the sticky cones, and each nut is precious.

PIÑON PINE

CONE

PINE NUTS

Wuzzie takes a special winnowing basket and puts two big hand-fuls of nuts in it. Then she uses a small shovel to lift out small coals from the fire. Very carefully she places the coals on the nuts and begins to toss the basket quickly, over and over. This is so the basket and nuts don't burn. We smell the spicy fragrance of melting pitch as the nuts cook. She keeps bouncing them in the air, turning and turning them, and when she hears them begin to pop like popcorn, she knows the nuts are cooked. She uses her hands to flick the hot coals out of the basket. We all gasp! Wuzzie must have tough fingers to do that!

After all the coals are removed, Wuzzie puts the pine nuts on a flat board. She uses a different rock called a "huller" to crack the shells. It is flatter than the mano. Wuzzie is very careful with this rock. She wants to crack the shell without crushing the tiny nut inside. But Wuzzie is really an expert. She taps the shells gingerly so that hardly any of the nuts inside get smashed.

When all the shells are cracked, Wuzzie scoops the nuts and shells off the board back into the winnowing basket. Then she stands up and checks to see where the wind is coming from. She picks up the basket and turns her back to the wind, tossing the nuts and shells into the air. The breeze carries off the light broken shells. The nuts fall back into the basket. She tosses and tosses until almost all the shells are blown away. We are all amazed to see how Wuzzie can throw the nuts into the air without dropping any! Then, with a few puffs, she blows the few remaining shells out of the basket.

Now the pine nuts are ready for the second roasting. With her small shovel, Wuzzie places some fresh coals onto the nuts, which are now in a winnowing basket that she has dampened with water to keep it from burning. This time she moves even more quickly, shaking the basket to make sure the nuts and basket don't burn. She tosses them straight up, then sideways, then rolls them around and around in the basket. The nuts are getting black, covered with dust from the coals.

But wait!! I can't remember how she makes our favorite soup from these dirty black pine nuts. Peg smiles and says it is time for "Wuzzie's magic."

We all watch as Wuzzie grinds a handful of the blackened nuts on the metate. Then she sprinkles this dark flour with a bit of water, mixing it into a gray paste. She takes the paste in her hands and begins to rub it over the blackened nuts. It is magic! The paste picks up all the dirt and charcoal. The nuts turn white almost immediately! We are getting very close to having pine nut soup!

Next, Wuzzie wipes the metate clean with her hands and puts a few of the cleaned nuts on it. Then, carefully and slowly, she grinds them into flour and pushes it onto a piece of newspaper next to the metate. Pretty soon Wuzzie has a big mound of flour. She puts it into a pot over the fire and adds some water. She stirs the soup with a stick, cooking and stirring until it is like thick cream. After she takes it off the fire, Wuzzie pours it out onto a round clay platter to cool. She smiles as we all stick our fingers into it, over and over, until the platter is scraped clean. It is so delicious! I think Wuzzie likes making pine nut soup for us because she giggles as we fight over the last drops.

Pine Nut Dance and Songs

That night some of Wuzzie's friends come to camp to show us the pine nut dance. They are wearing buckskin dresses and pants. One man is wearing a large headdress with long eagle feathers in it. The eagle feathers are stiff and white and go over the top of his head all the way down his back. They are held together in a band with small soft multicolored feathers around his face.

By now, the sky has deepened to a soft purple. As the day gives way to night, a soft turquoise hue outlines the distant mountains. The evening cools, and the dancers move toward the campfire, singing a chant. It is a song to the pine nut trees. Peg tells us the song is to bring rain so the nut crop will be healthy and strong. They stand close to each other in a circle. Their shoulders are touching. When the singer starts, they move slowly to the left. They do a shuffle step around the fire for a long time. The sky is now dark, and the firelight flickers off the pines boughs overhead, and seems to be dancing with the circling figures. The dark night, the firelight, the smoke, and song seem to cast a spell. It gives me a feeling of mystery, and I can imagine dancers doing this same dance for hundreds of years. We watch without saying a word.

Finally the Paiutes ask us to join them. The dance looks really easy so we all want to try it. We join the dancers and learn the steps. We are so fooled!! Something that looks so simple turns out to be really hard. In about five minutes it feels like our legs are going to drop off.

After the dance they sing more songs for us. Then they show us a hand game so complicated that none of us can figure it out. It is fun seeing them playing and laughing with each other. Finally at bedtime I drift off to sleep wondering what marvelous things Wuzzie, our Paiute friend, will show us tomorrow.

Tules and Cattails

After breakfast the next morning Peg and Wuzzie bring a bunch of tules and cattails out of the camper. These plants grow in swamps. Peg says she has helped Wuzzie pull them before and it is hard work to free the plants and roots from the thick mud. To get these tules and cattails, Wuzzie and Jimmie George, her husband, have walked into the swamps near Stillwater. To pull them, they reach all the way down to the roots. They say it is important to get the

whole root. The Paiute people use every bit of the tule and cattail. That is why their tribe is called the "Cattail eaters." Then Wuzzie and Jimmie trudge through the mud and water to carry the heavy bundles out on their backs. I wish we could have been there to help.

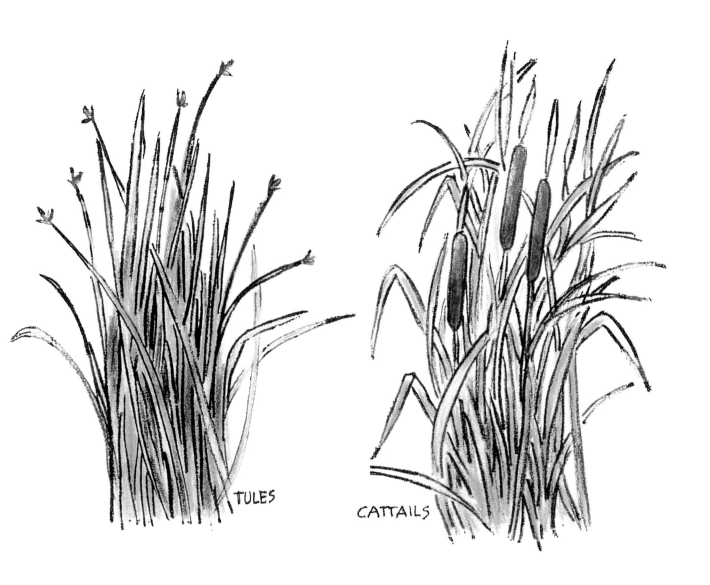

Tules and cattails look a lot alike. Tules have round stems with tiny air pockets inside. They have small brown seeds at the top. Cattails look like a brown velvet hot dog on a stick, and have long flat leaves.

Wuzzie shows us the whole tule root. The tender part can be eaten raw. With a sharp knife, she peels off a silken outer layer. Then she boils the root in a pot over the fire. She prepares the cattail roots the same way. Peg tells us that before Wuzzie had metal pots to cook in, she used a basket filled with water. She would cook the roots by putting hot rocks from the fire into the basket to do the cooking, since the basket could not go over the fire without burning.

This is a close-up view of a tule root. Can you see the tender part?

This is a close-up view of a cattail root. Can you see the difference? Have you ever tasted a tule root and cattail root salad? Peg and some of the campers did, and they liked it!

Mud Hen Egg Baskets

With the tules, Wuzzie shows us how she weaves a mud hen egg basket. It takes a lot of stalks to make the basket. It looks so easy when Wuzzie does it, but it is really hard for us campers. We must twist the tough reeds together in just the right direction to make it work, and it's hard to figure out. The counselors watch Wuzzie carefully, following each step, and then help us. The tules twist and bend around each other. She starts at the bottom, then weaves up the sides. With the leftover strands Wuzzie braids a handle. This basket can hold three dozen duck eggs, and only takes her an hour to make! It would take us forever. At home, Wuzzie just weaves herself a new basket when her old one wears out.

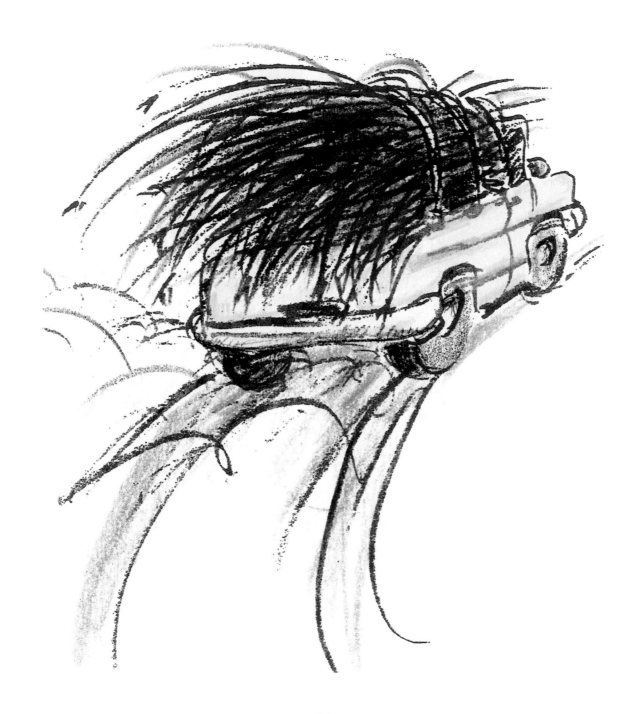

The Tule Boat

We get a wonderful surprise!! Peg tells us that a friend of Wuzzie's is coming after lunch with a load of tules and cattails. They are going to show us how to build a tule boat! Wow!!!

We hurry off to lunch, and are told we can even skip rest time today. The tule boat will take the whole afternoon to build. We are just finishing our cheese sandwiches and juice when we see an old yellow truck rumbling up the driveway, stirring up thick clouds of dust. It is loaded with big tules and cattails that are longer than I am tall.

Wuzzie's friend parks near the swimming pool and starts unloading onto the lawn. We all race across the camp to help. These tules are much larger than the ones we had for baskets. Under the tules are some cattail leaves. These are for making rope to tie the boat together. Wuzzie's friend John begins by soaking the cattails in the swimming pool. John tells us that this will make them more pliable to work with. Then they place two big bundles of tules side by side. When the cattail leaves are well soaked, Wuzzie and John twist them together into a strong rope. Cattails are stronger than tules for tying. Tules are better than cattails for floating. They make great partners in the construction of a tule boat.

After the rope is made, we get to help tie the bundles together. First we tie the two bundles separately. They look like huge cigars. They are fat on one end and narrow at the other. The boat will be about eight feet long.

Then we tie the two large bundles together. This takes a lot of rope! Peg has brought some heavy twine to help out, because it would take too long to make enough rope out of cattails.

At the front of the boat ... the narrow end ... Wuzzie and John pull the tules into a point that curves up. They tie it securely into place. This keeps water out of the boat.

Now we use more cattails to make smaller bundles. We tie these onto the top edges of the two big bundles. Tule boats are used to collect mud hen eggs in the swamps, and the top bundles act like holders to keep the eggs and the baskets from sliding off the boat. They use cattails for this because they are stronger than tules.

At last the boat is finished. It has taken us about four hours. We can't wait to see if it will float! Can we test it out in the swimming pool? Peg says yes, but we need to rinse it off first. The boat was covered with leaves and grass from the lawn, so we spray it clean with the garden hose. Wuzzie and John watch my friend Jesse and me carry the boat to the pool. It is so light we have no trouble lifting it. Then ... kersplosh!! In it goes.

It looks beautiful!! And ... it floats!!!

"Get in! Get in!" Everybody is shouting!!

I climb in very carefully. I don't want to tip over. The boat doesn't sink. It feels good. John hands me a pole to push the boat around with. I imagine myself exploring in the swamps looking for mud hen eggs. Everyone waits impatiently to take a turn in the boat. It is strong and sturdy and doesn't fall apart.

That afternoon we load the boat into one of the camp trucks. Peg and Wuzzie lead us to a place just outside Carson City, on the Carson River. We go where the river is wide but not very deep or swift. Clumps of brush dot the land along the sandy shore. We launch the boat again, and take turns floating on the river. It's hard to make it go where we want with only a pole to push with. Wuzzie and John stand on the shore and laugh as we struggle with the boat. It is so much fun that we play until dinnertime.

Then, sadly, after two wonderful days, we have to say goodbye to Wuzzie, so Peg can take her back to her home in Stillwater.

We all give a big cheer to Wuzzie and John for building this amazing tule boat for us.

We'll remember them as we play with the boat in the swimming pool. Maybe we can even take it to the river again before camp is over and we all have to go home again.

I love it when Wuzzie comes to camp!!!

How Wuzzie Worked

Wuzzie is a Paiute Indian. She is between seventy and eighty years old. This book is about some of the ways she got food. She lives in Nevada.

Eric's illustration of Wuzzie winnowing pinenuts.

Wuzzie George, circa 1964

Eric (1953-2005) winnowing pinenuts the way
Wuzzie taught him as a camper.

Peg Wheat and her dog, Silver

Pinenut forest, Nevada   Photos by Nancy Raven

Reviews

As an artist, writer and member of the California Indian community, I would like to strongly recommend Nancy Raven's Wuzzie Comes to Camp. The story of Wuzzie is beautiful in its simplicity and refreshing in its forthrightness. The focus is on Wuzzie and the knowledge she carried and shared. What I appreciated right away is that this is the telling of an actual experience — it is authentic.

I am absolutely in love with the illustrations! They convey the beauty and skill of the Paiute woman. They're rich in both color and content. They're fun, they're full of life. Surely this wonderful book will educate and delight — and be a lasting tribute to traditional knowledge.

Linda Yamane, Rumsien Ohlone

I have taught elementary school for over 38 years, most recently third and fourth grades, and find Nancy Raven's book about Wuzzie George a beautiful and informative childrens' book. Raven's sketches and paintings bring to life Wuzzie's warm focus, her strong, careful hands, and the young campers intent on Wuzzie's work. As a teacher of third and fourth graders I strive to give my students meaningful experiences when learning about Native Americans. Raven's book would truly enhance their study of California and Nevada Indians and the ways they lived. It is engaging and specific, truly a treasure.

Charlotte Roberts, Carmel River School, Carmel, CA

I am an elementary school teacher, and have taught in the public schools in Monterey, California, for 38 years. I've taught every grade second through sixth, and have a great appreciation of literature that acquaints children with people and places in the real world. I have been in search for good quality books about Native Americans. The social studies curriculum for the third grade concerns the study of Native Americans and how they lived.

Nancy Raven's excellent book Wuzzie Comes to Camp will delight children with the descriptions of how Native Americans lived. Our third grade students have hands-on experiences using natural materials that Native Americans used for food, house and boat building, and cloth making. Nancy's book will enrich that experience. I look forward to sharing this book with my students.

Carol Collin, Bay View School, Monterey, CA

About Wuzzie George

Wuzzie Dick George, her first name an Anglicization of her Northern Paiute given name, died in 1984 after a long and productive life. She married a medicine man whose contributions to their community are also well known, and together they raised a large family. In her lifetime stretching over more than a century Wuzzie George learned and plied an enormous array of traditional skills, which she taught to her own family and to other interested people. Through her work with anthropologist Margaret Wheat, much of her great knowledge has been recorded in books, articles, and film. As one token of the esteem in which Wuzzie George is held, the state of Nevada adopted a resolution in 1995 "commending Wuzzie Dick George and her family for preserving the traditions of the Northern Paiute People of the Stillwater Marsh."

But perhaps less well known is the impact she had on a group of young children at a summer camp in the mountains. Year after year, starting in the 1960s when Wuzzie was already in her 80s, the children, and their counselors as well, had the pleasure of learning from Wuzzie about the making of such traditional items as pine nut soup and rice grass and buckwheat mush, tule baskets, and tule boats. They had the honor of seeing the Paiute pine nut dance and hand game.

It is likely that those children, now middle-aged men and women, still retain strong memories of those events. Certainly one of their counselors does. Nancy Raven, a well-known singer of children's folksongs and a talented artist, was a counselor at that camp. The rediscovery of a child's journal rekindled her own fond memories of Wuzzie, and inspired this book. Raven's lovely illustrations evoke the sense of wonder that the children must have had in this very special experience of knowing and learning from Wuzzie George.

Leanne Hinton, professor emerita
University of California at Berkeley

Printed in the United States
By Bookmasters